Niagara Falls: The History of North America's Most Famous Waterfalls

By Charles River Editors

An aerial view of Niagara Falls

About Charles River Editors

Charles River Editors provides superior editing and original writing services across the digital publishing industry, with the expertise to create digital content for publishers across a vast range of subject matter. In addition to providing original digital content for third party publishers, we also republish civilization's greatest literary works, bringing them to new generations of readers via ebooks.

Sign up here to receive updates about free books as we publish them, and visit Our Kindle Author Page to browse today's free promotions and our most recently published Kindle titles.

Introduction

Horseshoe Falls from the Canadian side

Niagara Falls

"All trembling, I reached the Falls of Niagara, and oh, what a scene! My blood shudders still, although I am not a coward, at the grandeur of the Creator's power; and I gazed motionless on this new display of the irresistible force of one of His elements." - John James Audubon

"It's Niagara Falls. It's one of the most beautiful natural wonders in the world. Who wouldn't want to walk across it?" - Nik Wallenda

North America is full of natural wonders, but few inspire as much awe as Niagara Falls, the continent's most famous waterfalls. Comprised of three separate waterfalls (Horseshoe Falls, American Falls, and Bridal Veil Falls), Niagara's falls can boast of the fastest flow rate in the world, dropping 6 million cubic feet of water every minute from as high as 185 feet. Situated on the border between the United States and Canada, Niagara Falls is not just a prime tourist spot but a source of hydroelectric power that attracted scientists like Nikola Tesla who hoped to harness the waterfalls' energy. In fact, Niagara Falls is so powerful that it is eroding the ground under it, to the extent that it will cease to exist in about 50,000 years.

Niagara Falls is a byproduct of glaciers receding about 10,000 years ago, and it has been amazing people for as long as the area has been inhabited. It's widely believed Niagara is a word derived from the Mohawk tribe, but the most famous people now associated with the waterfalls are those who have dared to ride down the falls one way or another. The falls have seen both amateurs and professional stuntmen ride over it in barrels, some successfully and others fatally, and a local museum has even preserved some of the barrels used in the attempts. Just as daringly, others have tried to walk tightropes across the falls.

Niagara Falls: The History of North America's Most Famous Waterfalls traces the history of the region and its establishment as a park. Along with pictures of important people, places, and events, you will learn about Yosemite like never before, in no time at all.

Niagara Falls: The History of North America's Most Famous Waterfalls
About Charles River Editors
Introduction
   Chapter 1: The Neck
   Chapter 2: Their Roar is Around Me
   Chapter 3: An Infinite Quantity of Fresh Water
   Chapter 4: Positions
   Chapter 5: A Perpetual Creation
   Chapter 6: The Whirlwind of Spray
   Chapter 7: Stunts
   Chapter 8: Recent History
   Online Resources
   Bibliography

Chapter 1: The Neck

Alvan Fisher's *A General View of the Falls of Niagara* **(1820)**

Frederic Edwin Church's *Niagara Falls* **(1857)**

"Niagara Falls. This name is Mohawk. It means, according to Mrs. Kerr, the neck; the term being first applied to the portage or neck of land, between lakes Erie and Ontario. By referring to Mr. Elliott's vocabulary, (chapter xi) it will be seen that the human neck, that is, according to the concrete vocabulary, his neck, is onyara. Red Jacket pronounced the word Niagara to me, in the spring of 1820, as if written O-ne-au-ga-rah." - Henry Schoolcraft, author of *Notes on the Iroquois* (1847)

When Europeans began exploring North America in the early 17th century, they were often surprised and even amazed by what they saw. However, among the French tramping through the wild regions in what is now upstate New York, a rumor was passed around of giant waterfall unlike anything else ever seen. In 1604, French explorer Samuel de Champlain became the first European to write about what would soon be known as Niagara Falls after learning of it during his exploration of Lake Ontario. Though he never saw the falls himself, he was able to appreciate the tales told by the Native Americans in the area and recorded what they told him about the falls. Later, in 1632, he was even able to create a reasonably accurate map based on what he had heard: "After this, they enter a very large lake, some three hundred leagues in length. Proceeding some hundred leagues in this lake, they come to a very large island, beyond which the water is good; but that, upon going some hundred leagues farther, the water has become somewhat bad, and, upon reaching the end of the lake, it is perfectly salt. That there is a fall about a league wide, where a very large mass of water falls into said lake; that, when this fall is passed, one sees no more land on either side, but only a sea so large that they have never seen the end of it, nor heard that any one has; that the sun sets on the right of this lake, at the entrance to which there is a river extending towards the Algonquins, and another towards the Iroquois, by way of which they go to war."

Little more was known about the falls until 1669, when Frenchman Rene Brehan de Galinée noted, "This outlet contains, at a distance of ten or twelve leagues, from its mouth in Lake Ontario, one of the finest cataracts or water-falls in the world: for all the Indians to whom I have spoken about it said the river fell in that place from a rock higher than the tallest pine trees, that is, about two hundred feet. In fact, we heard it from where we were. But this fall gives such impulse to the water that, although we were ten or twelve leagues away, the water is so rapid that one can with great difficulty row up against it.... With a roar that is heard not only from the place where we were ten to twelve leagues distant but actually the other side of Lake Ontario, opposite this mouth from which M. Trouvé told me he heard it."

Galinée hadn't actually seen the waterfalls, and neither did Le Sieur Gendron, but Gendron also recorded what he heard during his exploration of North America: "Almost south of the Neuter Nation is a large lake, almost 200 leagues in circumference, called Erie, which is formed from the discharge of the Fresh Water Sea (Lake Huron) and which falls from a terrible height into a third lake called Ontario, which we call Lake St. Louis. The spray of these waters rebounding from the foot of certain large rocks in that place, forms a stone, or rather a petrified salt, of a yellowish color and of admirable virtue for the curing of sores, fistules, and malign ulcers. In this horrible place there dwell also certain savages who live only on the elks, stags, wild cows, and other kinds of game which the rapids carry along and cast among these rocks where they (the savages) take them without hunting in larger numbers than suffices for their needs and the entertainment of the travelers with whom they deal in these Erie stones so called because of this lake, so that they take them along and distribute them afterwards among other nations."

By this time, the New World, especially its northern environs, were a source of great interest to Europe, and the Catholic Church had begun to send priests over to attempt to convert the natives of this new land. One of these priests, Father Louis Hennepin, had the honor of being the first European to see the falls and record what it looked like. After seeing Niagara Falls in 1678, he published a record of his travels (and an illustration of the waterfalls) in 1697.

"On the 6th (December, 1678), St. Nicholas day, we entered the beautiful river Niagara, which no bark had ever yet entered…Four leagues from Lake Frontenac there is an incredible Cataract or Waterfall, which has no equal. The Niagara River near this place is only the eighth of a league wide, but it is very deep in places, and so rapid above the great fall, that it hurries down all the animals which try to cross it, without a single one being able to withstand its current. They plunge down a height of more than five hundred feet, and its fall is composed of two sheets of water and a cascade, with an island sloping down. In the middle these waters foam and boil in a fearful manner. They thunder continually, and when the wind blows in a southerly direction, the noise which they make is heard for from more than fifteen leagues. Four leagues from this cataract or fall, the Niagara River rushes with extraordinary rapidity especially for two leagues into Lake Frontenac. It is during these two leagues that goods are carried. There is a very fine road, very little wood, and almost all prairies mingled with some oaks and firs, on both banks of the river, which are of a height that inspire fear when you look down…

"Betwixt the Lake Ontario and Erie, there is a vast and prodigious Cadence of Water which falls down after a surprising and astonishing manner, insomuch that the Universe does not afford it's parallel. Tis true, Italy and Suedland boast some such Things; but we may well say they are but sorry Patterns, when compared to this of which we now speak. At the foot of this horrible Precipice, we meet with the River Niagara, which is not above a quarter of a League broad, but is wonderfully deep in some places. It is so rapid above this Descent, that it violently hurries down the wild Beasts while endeavoring to pass it to feed on the other side, they not being able to withstand the force of its Current, which inevitably casts them above Six hundred foot high...This wonderful Downfall is compounded of two great Cross-streams of Water, and two Falls, with an Isle sloping along the middle of it. the Waters which fall from this horrible Precipice, do foam and boil after the most hideous manner imaginable, making an outrageous Noise, more terrible than that of Thunder; for when the Wind blows out of the South, their dismal roaring may be heard more than Fifteen Leagues off...The River Niagara having thrown itself down this incredible Precipice, continues its impetuous course for two Leagues together, to the great Rock above-mentioned [Queenston Heights], with an inexpressible rapidity: But having past that, its impetuosity relents, gliding along more gently for two other Leagues, till it arrive at Lake Frontenac (Lake Ontario)...

"I could not conceive how it came to pass, that four great Lakes, the least of which is 400 Leagues in compass, should empty themselves one into another, and then all centre and discharge themselves at this Great Fall, and yet not drown [a] good part of America. What is yet more surprising, the Ground from the Mouth of the Lake Erie, down to the Great Fall, appears almost level and flat. 'Tis scarce discernable that there is the least Rise or Fall for six Leagues together: The more than ordinary swiftness of the Stream, is the only thing that makes it be observed. And that which makes it yet the stranger is, That for two Leagues together below the Fall, towards the Lake Ontario, or Frontenac, the Lands are as level as they are above it towards the Lake of Erie. Our Surprise was still greater, when we observed there were no Mountains within two good Leagues of this Cascade; and yet the vast quantity of Water which is discharged by these four fresh Seas, stops or centers here, and so falls about six hundred Foot down into a Gulf, which one cannot look upon without Horror. Two other great Outlets, or Falls of Water, which are on the two sides of a small sloping Island, which is in the midst, fall gently and without noise, and so glide away quietly enough: But when this prodigious quantity of Water, of which I speak, comes to fall, there is such a din, and such a noise, that is more deafening than the loudest Thunder. The rebounding of these Waters is so great, that a sort of Cloud arises from the Foam of it, which are seen hanging over this Abyss even at Noon-day, when the Sun is at its height. In the midst of Summer, when the Weather is hottest, they arise above the tallest Firs, and other great Trees, which grow in the sloping Island which make the two Falls of Water that I spoke of."

Hennepin then went on to describe in surprising detail the land and rivers around the falls, giving some of first clear measurements of their features. Though some of his observations have since been questioned, they nonetheless offer surprising details consistent with more recent observations. "From the Mouth of the Lake Erie to the Great Fall, are reckoned six Leagues, as I have said, which is the continuation of the Great River of St. Lawrence, which arises out of the four Lakes above-mentioned. The River, you must needs think, is very rapid for these six Leagues, because of the vast Discharge of Waters which fall into it out of the said Lakes. The Lands, which lie on both sides of it to the East and West, are all level from the Lake Erie to the Great Fall. Its Banks are not steep; on the contrary, the Water is almost always level with the

Land. 'Tis certain, that the Ground towards the Fall is lower, by the more than ordinary swiftness of the Stream; and yet 'tis not perceivable to the Eye for the six Leagues above said. After it has run thus violently for six Leagues, it meets with a small sloping Island, about half a quarter of a League long, and near three hundred Foot broad, as well as one can guess by the Eye; for it is impossible to come at it in a Canoe of Bark, the Waters run with that force. The Isle is full of Cedar and Fir; but the Land of it lies no higher than that on the Banks of the River. It seems to be all level, even as far as the two great Cascades that make the Main Fall."

One of the things that struck Hennepin was the difference in the way in which the waters flowed on the different sides of the falls. He explained:

"The two sides of the Channels, which are made by the Isle, and run on both sides of it, overflow almost the very Surface of the Earth of the said Isle, as well as the Land that lies on the Banks of the River to the East and West, as it runs South and North. But we must observe, that at the end of the Isle, on the side of the two great Falls, there is a sloping Rock which reaches as far as the Great Gulf, into which the said Waters fall; and yet the Rock is not at all wetted by the two Cascades which fall on both sides, because the two Torrents which are made by the Isle, throw themselves with a prodigious force, one towards the East, and the other towards the West, from off the end of the Isle, where the Great Fall of all is. After then these two Torrents have thus run by the two sides of the Isle, they cast their Waters all of a sudden down into the Gulf by two Great Falls; which Waters are pushed so violently on by their own Weight, and so sustained by the swiftness of the motion, that they don't wet the Rock in the least. And here it is that they tumble down into an Abyss above 600 Foot in depth…

"The Waters that flow on the side of the East, do not throw themselves with that violence as those that fall on the West. The reason is, because the Rock at the end of the Island, rises something more on this side, than it does on the West; and so the Waters being supported by it somewhat longer than they are on the other side, are carried the smoother off: But on the West the Rock sloping more, the Waters, for want of a Support, become the sooner broke, and fall with the greater precipitation. Another reason is, the Lands that lie on the West are lower than those that lie on the East. We also observed, that the Waters of the Fall, that is to the West, made a sort of a square Figure as they fell, which made a third Cascade, less than the other two, which fell betwixt the South and North. And because there is a rising Ground which lies before those two Cascades to the North, the Gulf is much larger there than to the East. Moreover, we must observe, that from the rising ground that lies over against the two last Falls which are on the West of the main Fall, one may go down as far as the bottom of this terrible Gulf. The Author of this Discovery was down there, the more narrowly to observe the Fall of these prodigious Cascades. From hence we could discover a Spot of Ground, which lay under the Fall of Water which is to the East, big enough for four Coaches to drive a breast without being wet; but because the Ground, which is to the East of the sloping Rock, where the first Fall empties itself into the Gulf, is very steep, and almost perpendicular, 'tis impossible for a Man to get down on that side, into the Place where the four Coaches may go a-breast, or to make his way through such a quantity of Water as falls towards the Gulf: So that 'tis very probable, that to this dry Place it is that the Rattle-Snakes retire, by certain Passages which they find underground."

Of course, the top of the falls, amazing as they were, were nothing compared to the area below, where the massive amount of water splashes down. "From the end then of this Island it is, that these two Great Falls of Waters, as also the third but now mentioned, throw themselves, after a most surprising manner, down into a dreadful Gulf six hundred Foot and more in depth. I have already said, that the Waters which Discharge themselves at the Cascade to the East, fall with lesser force; whereas those to the West tumble all at once, making two Cascades; one moderate, the other very violent and strong, which at last make a kind of Crochet, or square Figure, falling from South to North, and West to East. After this, they rejoin the Waters of the other Cascade that falls to the East, and so tumble down altogether, though unequally, into the Gulf, with all the violence that can be imagined, from a Fall of six hundred Foot, which makes the most Beautiful, and at the same time most Frightful Cascade in the World. After these Waters have thus discharged themselves into this dreadful Gulf, they begin to resume their Course, and continue the great River of St. Lawrence for two Leagues, as far as the three Mountains which are on the East of the River, and the great Rock which is on the West, and lifts itself three Fathoms above the Waters, or thereabouts. The Gulf into which these Waters are discharged continues itself thus two Leagues together, between a Chain of Rocks, flowing with a prodigious Torrent, which is bridled and kept in by the Rocks that lie on each side of the River."

Like those before and after him, Hennepin was struck by the incredible noise the waters made, and the way in which they returned again to the rivers at the bottom of the falls. "Into this Gulf it is, that these several Cascades empty themselves, with a violence equal to the height from whence they fall, and the quantity of Waters, which they discharge. Hence arise those deafening Sounds, that dreadful roaring and bellowing of the Waters which drown the loudest Thunder, as also the perpetual Mists that hang over the Gulf, and rise above the tallest Pines that are in the little Isle so often mentioned. After a Channel is again made at the bottom of this dreadful Fall by the Chain of Rocks, and filled by that prodigious quantity of Waters which are continually falling, the River of St. Lawrence resumes its Course: But with that violence, and his Waters beat against the Rocks with so prodigious a force, that 'tis impossible to pass even in a Canoe of Bark. … These Rocks, as also the prodigious Torrent, last for two Leagues; that is, from the great Fall, to the three Mountains and great Rock: But then it begins insensibly to abate, and the Land to be again almost on a level with the Water; and so it continues as far as the Lake Ontario, or Frontenac. When one stands near the Fall, and looks down into this most dreadful Gulf, one is seized with Horror, and the Head turns round, so that one cannot look long or steadfastly upon it. But this vast Deluge beginning insensibly to abate, and even to fall to nothing about the three Mountains, the Waters of the River St. Lawrence begin to glide more gently along, and to be almost upon a level with the Lands; so that it becomes navigable again, as far as the Lake Frontenac."

A year after Hennepin's exploration, Henry de Tonty visited the falls and wrote that "it throws off vapor which may be seen at a distance of sixteen (16) leagues and it may be heard at the same distance when it is calm."

Chapter 2: Their Roar is Around Me

Louis Rémy Mignot's *Niagara* (circa 1866)

Arthur Parton's *Niagara Falls* (circa 1880)

"Their roar is around me. I am on the brink Of the great waters—and their anthem voice Goes up amid the rainbow and the mist." – Grenville Mellen, "Niagara" (1839)

The area around Niagara Falls would remain in native and French hands for the next several decades, allowing other French explorers to see the waterfalls and describe them to people back home. For example, Pierre François Xavier De Charlevoix, one of the most famous Jesuit writers of the 18th century, described the falls in 1721 while writing to the Duchess of Lesdiguières:

> "The officers having departed, I ascended those frightful mountains, in order to visit the famous Fall of Niagara, above which I was to take water; this is a journey of three leagues, though formerly five; because the way then lay by the other, that is, the west-side of the river, and also because the place for embarking lay full two leagues above the Fall. But there has since been found, on the left, at the distance of half a quarter of a league from this cataract, a creek, where the current is not perceivable, and consequently a place where one may take water without danger...
>
> "Now, Madam, we must acknowledge, that nothing but zeal for the public good could possibly induce an officer to remain in such a country as this, than which a wilder and more frightful is not to be seen. On the one side you see just under your

feet, and as it were at the bottom of an abyss, a great river, but which in this place is like a torrent by its rapidity, by the whirlpools formed by a thousand rocks, through which it with difficulty finds a passage, and by the foam with which it is always covered; on the other the view is confined by three mountains placed one over the other, and whereof the last hides itself in the clouds. This would have been a very proper scene for the poets to make the Titans attempt to scale the heavens. In a word, on whatever side you turn your eyes, you discover nothing which does not inspire a secret horror. You have, however, but a very short way to go, to behold a very different prospect. Behind those uncultivated and uninhabitable mountains, you enjoy the sight of a rich country, magnificent forests, beautiful and fruitful hills; you breathe the purest air, under the mildest and most temperate climate imaginable, situated between two lakes the least of which is two hundred and fifty leagues in circuit."

Pierre Francois Xavier de Charlevoix

With the precision and sense of accuracy common to members of the Jesuit order, Charlevoix took exception to mistakes made in past accounts and was determined to provide as precise a set of measurements as possible. "My first care, after my arrival, was to visit the noblest cascade perhaps in the world; but I presently found the baron de la Hontan had committed such a mistake with respect to its height and figure, as to give grounds to believe he had never seen it. It is certain, that if you measure its height by that of the three mountains, you are obliged to climb to get at it, it does not come much short of what the map of M. Deslisle makes it; that is, six hundred feet, having certainly gone into this paradox, either, on the faith of the baron de la Hontan or Father Hennepin; but after I arrived at the summit of the third mountain, I observed, that in the space of three leagues, which I had to walk before I came to this piece of water, though you are sometimes obliged to ascend, you must yet descend still more, a circumstance to which travelers seem not to have sufficiently attended. As it is impossible to approach it but on one side only, and consequently to see it, excepting in profile, or sideways; it is no easy matter to measure its height with instruments. It, has, however, been attempted by means of a pole tied to a long line, and after many repeated trials, it has been found only one hundred and fifteen, or one hundred and twenty feet high. But it is impossible to be sure that the pole has not been stopped by some projecting rock; for though it was always drawn up wet, as well as the end of the line to which it was tied, this proves nothing at all, as the water which precipitates itself from the mountain, rises very high in foam. For my own part, after having examined it on all sides, where it could be viewed to the greatest advantage, I am inclined to think we cannot allow it less than a hundred and forty, or fifty feet."

Charlevoix also became one of the first writers to describe the shape of the falls as they wrapped around the edge of the mountains. "As to its figure, it is in the shape of a horseshoe, and is about four hundred paces in circumference; it is divided into two, exactly in the middle, by a very narrow island, half a quarter of a league long. It is true, those two parts very soon unite; that on my side, and which I could only have a side view of, has several branches which project from the body of the cascade, but that which I viewed in front, appeared to me quite entire. The baron de la Hontan mentions a torrent, which if this author has not invented it, must certainly fall through some channel on the melting of the snows. You may easily guess, Madam, that a great way below this Fall, the river still retains strong marks of so violent a shock; accordingly, it becomes only navigable three leagues below, and exactly at the place which M. de Joncaire has chosen for his residence [now Lewiston]. It should by right be equally unnavigable above it, since the river falls perpendicular the whole space of its breadth. But besides the island, which divides it into two, several rocks which are scattered up and down above it, abate much of the rapidity of the stream; it is notwithstanding so very strong, that ten or twelve Outaways trying to cross over to the island to shun the Iroquoise who were in pursuit of them, were drawn into the precipice, in spite of all their efforts to preserve themselves."

Charlevoix even provided some of the most detailed accounts of the wildlife in and around the falls, calling into question some of the more outlandish claims made by earlier explorers. "I have heard say that the fish that happen to be entangled in the current, fall dead into the river, and that the Indians of those parts were considerably advantaged by them; but I saw nothing of this sort. I was also told, that the birds that attempted to fly over were sometimes caught in the whirlwind formed, by the violence of the torrent. But I observed quite the contrary, for I saw small birds flying very low, and exactly over the Fall, which yet cleared their passage very well. This sheet of water falls upon a rock, and there are two reasons which induce me to believe, that it has either found, or perhaps in time hollowed out a cavern of considerable depth. The first is, that the noise it makes is very hollow, resembling that of thunder at a distance. You can scarce hear it at M. de Joncaire's, and what you hear in this place, may possibly be only that of the whirlpools caused by the rocks, which fill the bed of the river as far as this. And so much the rather as above the cataract, you do not hear it near so far. The second is, that nothing has ever been seen again that has once fallen over it, not even the wrecks of the canoe of the Outaways, I mentioned just now. . . . Besides I perceived no mist above it, but from behind, at a distance, one would take it for smoke, and there is no person who would not be deceived with it, if he came insight of the isle, without having been told before hand that there was so surprising a cataract in this place. The soil of the three leagues I had to walk a foot to get hither, and which is called the carrying-place of Niagara, seems very indifferent; it is even very ill-wooded, and you cannot walk ten paces without treading on ant-hills, or meeting with rattlesnakes, especially during the heat of the day."

Chapter 3: An Infinite Quantity of Fresh Water

William Morris Hunt's *Niagara Falls* (1878)

Thomas Cole's *Distant View of Niagara Falls* (1830)

"The River of St. Lawrence or Canada, receives in these Parts an Infinite Quantity of fresh Water from the four great Lakes, the Lake Huron, the upper Lake, the Lake of the Illinois, and the Lake Erie or of the Cat, which may properly be called little fresh Water Seas. This great Deluge of Water tumbling furiously over the greatest and most dreadful Heap in the World, an infinite Number of Fish take a great Delight to spawn here, and as it were suffocate here, because they cannot get over this huge Cataract: So that the Quantity taken here is incredible. A Gentleman who was Travelling this Part, went to see this Heap, which comes from a River in the North, and falls into a great Basin of Lake Outario, big enough to hold a Hundred Men of War, being there he taught the Natives to catch Fish with their Hands, by causing Trees to be cut down in the Spring, and to be rolled to the Bank of the River, so that he might be upon them without wetting himself…" - The first English account of the Niagara Falls, published in London in 1710.

In 1721, Paul Dudley, an associate justice with the Superior Court of Judicature in Massachusetts, recorded information he received from a Frenchman from Canada named Borassaw. He took it upon himself to interrogate his witness carefully and to challenge many of the claims made by earlier explorers, especially Hennepin.

> "The falls of Niagara are formed by a vast ledge or precipice of solid rock, lying across the whole breadth of the river, a little before it empties itself into, or forms the Lake Ontario. M. Borassaw says, that in the spring 1722 (should be 1721), the governor of Canada ordered his son, with three other officers, to survey the Niagara, and take the exact height of the cataract, which they accordingly did with a stone of half a hundred weight, and a large cod-line and found it on a perpendicular no more than 26 fathoms.... This differs very much from the account Father Hennepin has given to that cataract; for he makes it 100 fathoms, and our modern maps from him, as I suppose, mark it 600 feet; but I believe Hennepin never measured it, and there is no guessing at such things. When I objected Hennepin's account of those falls to M. Borassaw, he replied, that accordingly everybody had depended on it as right, until the late survey. On further discourse he acknowledged, that below the cataract, for a great way, there were numbers of small ledges or stairs across the river, that lowered it still more and more, till it came to a level; so that if all the descents be put together, he does not know but that the difference of the water above the falls and the level below, may come up to Father Hennepin; but the strict and proper cataract on a perpendicular is no more than 26 fathoms, or 156 feet, which yet is a prodigious thing, and what the world I suppose cannot parallel, considering the size of the river, being near a quarter of an English mile broad, and very deep water."

Dudley was also especially interested in fish around the river and admitted that he found what might otherwise be considered outlandish claims about their size to be believable.

> "Several other things M. Borassaw set me right in, as to the falls of Niagara. Particularly it has been said, that the cataract makes such a prodigious noise, that people cannot hear each other speak at some miles distances; whereas he affirms, that you may converse together close by it. I have also heard it positively asserted, that the shoot of the river, when it comes to the precipice, was with such force, that men and horse might march under the body of the river without being wet; this also he utterly denies, and says the water falls in a manner right down. What he observed farther to me was, that the mist or shower which the falls make, is so extraordinary, as to be seen at five leagues distance, and rise as high as the common clouds. In this brume or cloud, when the sun shines, you have always a glorious rainbow. That the river itself, which is there called the river Niagara, is much narrower at the falls than either above or below; and that from below there is no coming nearer the falls by water than about six English miles, the torrent is so rapid, and having such terrible whirlpools. He confirms Father Hennepin's...account of the large trouts of those lakes, and solemnly affirmed there was one taken lately, that

weighed 86 lb. which I am rather inclined to believe, on the general rule, that fish are according to the waters. To confirm which, a very worthy minister affirmed, that he saw a pike taken in a Canada river, and carried on a pole between two men, that measured five feet ten inches in length, and proportionately thick."

Several decades later, Joseph Pierre de Bonnecamps visited Niagara Falls in 1749 and described it "as having a vertical fall of one hundred and thirty-three (133) feet, half-ellipsed divided near the middle by a little island [and a] "width of…perhaps 3/8 of a league." Peter Kalm, a botanist who originally came to North America from Sweden, wrote in 1750, "I doubt not but you have a desire to learn the exact height of this great fall. Father Hennepin, you know, calls it 600 feet perpendicular; but he has gained little credit in Canada; the name of honor they give him here, is un grand Menteur, or the great Liar; he writes of what he saw in places where he never was. 'Tis true he saw this fall: But as it is the way of some travelers to magnify everything, so has he done with regard to the fall of Niagara....Since Father Hennepin's time, this fall, in all the accounts that have been given of it, has grown less and less; and those who have measured it with mathematical instruments find the perpendicular fall of the water to be exactly 137 feet.... You may remember, to what great distance Hennepin says the noise of this fall may be heard. All the gentlemen who were with me agreed, that the farthest one can hear it, is 15 leagues, and that very seldom.... Sometimes 'tis said, the fall makes much greater noise than at other times; and this is looked on as a certain mark of approaching bad weather, or rain; the Indians here hold it always as a sure sign. When I was there, it did not make an extraordinary great noise: Just by the fall, we could easily hear what each other said, without speaking much louder than the common when conversing in other places. I do not know how others found so great a noise here; perhaps it was at certain times, as above mentioned."

Fascinated with the noise the great falls made, Kalm continued, "When the air is quite calm, you can hear it to Fort Niagara: but seldom at other times, because when the wind blows, the waves of Lake Ontario make too much noise there against the shore - They informed me, that when that when they hear at the Fort the noise of the Fall, louder than ordinary, they are sure a north - east wind will follow, which never fails: this seems wonderful, as the fall is south - west from the Fort: and one would imagine it to be a rather sign of a contrary wind. Sometimes 'tis said, the Fall makes a much greater noise than at other times; and this looked upon as a certain mark of approaching bad weather or rain: the Indians here hold it always for a sure sign - When I was there..."

As the years passed, more and more explorers made their way to the falls, and in 1766 Captain Jonathan Carver wrote down some of his observations of the area: "This Lake (Erie) discharges its waters at the northeast end, into the River Niagara, which runs north and south, and is about thirty-six miles in length; from whence it falls into Lake Ontario. At the entrance of this river, on its eastern shore, lies Fort Niagara; and, about eighteen miles further up, those remarkable Falls which are esteemed one of the most extraordinary productions of nature at present known. As these have been visited by so many travelers, and so frequently described, I shall omit giving a particular description of them, and only observe, that the waters by which they are supplied, after taking their rise near two thousand miles to the northwest, and passing through the Lakes Superior, Michigan, Huron, and Erie, during which they have been receiving constant accumulations, at length rush down a stupendous precipice of one hundred and forty feet perpendicular; and in a strong rapid, that extends to the distance of eight or nine miles below, fall nearly as much more: this River soon after empties itself into Lake Ontario. The noise of these Falls might be heard an amazing way. I could plainly distinguish them in a calm morning more than twenty miles. Others have said that at particular times, and when the wind sits fair, the sound of them reaches fifteen leagues."

In 1789, Ann Powell became one of the first female writers to write about the falls: "The fort [Niagara] is by no means pleasantly situated. It is built close upon the Lake, which gains upon its foundations so fast, that in a few years they must be overflowed. . . . The road was good, the weather charming, and this was the only opportunity we should have of seeing the Falls. All our party collected half a mile above the Falls, and walked down to them. I was in raptures all the way. The Falls I had heard of forever, but no one had mentioned the Rapids! For half a mile the river comes foaming down immense rocks, some of them forming cascades 30or 40 feet high! The banks are covered with woods, as are a number of Islands, some of them very high out of the water. One in the centre of the river, runs out into a point, and seems to divide the Falls, which would otherwise be quite across the river, into the form of a crescent. I believe no mind can form an idea of the immensity of the body of water, or the rapidity with which it hurries down. The height is 180 feet, and long before it reaches the bottom, it loses all appearance of a liquid. The spray rises like light summer clouds, and when the rays of the sun are reflected through it, they form innumerable rainbows, but the sun was not in a situation to show this effect when we were there. One thing I could find nobody to explain to me, which is, the stillness of the water at the bottom of the Falls; it is as smooth as a lake, for half a mile, deep and narrow, the banks very high and steep, with trees hanging over them. I was never before sensible of the power of scenery, nor did I suppose the eye could carry to the mind such strange emotions of pleasure, wonder and solemnity. For a time every other impression was erased from my memory! Had I been left to myself, I am convinced I should not have thought of moving whilst there was light to distinguish objects."

Chapter 4: Positions

"For the disappointment which is usually felt in gaining the first look of the falls, it is not difficult to account. We are accustomed to expect that the peculiar beauties of 'the mountain and the flood' should never be disconnected in the landscape, and are not prepared to find the falls of Niagara in the midst of a tract of country level to perfect deadness; a country where for miles around not a solitary hillock varies the surface, and nothing meets the eye but interminable forests of pine. The positions from which you must view the falls, and their vast semicircular width, detract most surprisingly from their apparent altitude. Add to all this, the unbridled scope in which imagination delights to riot, magnifying what is small and exaggerating what is great, and surely it will no longer be surprising that many, who take but a flying view of the wonders of Niagara, should depart utterly displeased that they are not still more wonderful." - John M. Duncan

An 1837 engraving of Niagara Falls

In the years following American independence, the United States and Canada established a sort of joint ownership of Niagara Falls that continues to this day. The area also began to attract more and more tourists, and in 1823, John M. Duncan published his account of the area in his book *Travels through part of the United States and Canada in 1818 and 1819.* In it, he took on the burning issue of the day, which was a concern that the falls might actually be receding. "It was on a beautiful morning that I last left Buffalo; the sky was clear and the air perfectly serene. Not a single cloud was seen upon the broad expanse, except in the northwest, on the very verge of the horizon, where two little fleecy specks appeared and disappeared at intervals; sometimes rising separately, and sometimes mingling their vapours. These were clouds of spray rising above the falls; perfectly conspicuous to the naked eye at a distance of twenty miles. The western bank of the Niagara has been settled for a considerable period; the land is of excellent quality, and a great part of it cleared and cultivated. It will no doubt be a long time, ere the whole landscape assume that unpicturesque commonplace, which is produced by ploughing and harrowing, levelling and enclosing; many an axe must be raised, and many a lofty pine-tree measure its length upon the ground, ere waving grain displace all the shaggy forests which stretch around. Time however, that silent but most innovating of reformers, is working wondrous changes on this western world; and his operations are nowhere so apparent as on the banks of navigable streams. In a few years, perhaps, the noise of the cataracts may be drowned in the busy hum of men; and the smoke of clustering towns, or more crowded cities, obscure on the horizon the clouds of spray, which at present tower without a rival."

By this time, the island so often mentioned in earlier accounts had been named Goat Island because John Stedman, an 18th century pioneer in the area, had once kept a herd of goats there. By the beginning of the 19th century, however, the goats were gone and the island had become a popular place from which to view the falls. Duncan wrote, "Nearly opposite the middle of Goat Island the channel of the rapid suddenly widens, encroaching with a considerable curvature upon the bank, as if a portion of the water sought to shun by a circuitous route its inevitable destiny. In this little bay, if it may be so called, are a number of islets covered with wood, and to all appearance securely anchored amid the brawling torrent: but before approaching them, you discover with surprise that the daring foot of man has ventured to descend the steep bank, to erect a cluster of mills, which dip their water wheels into the impetuous rapid. In my first visit I was quite alone, and piloted my way from the tavern to the edge of the precipitous bank, by the directions which I received from the landlord. Crossing afield or two, which slope from the road towards the river, a little below the falls, I reached a small distillery, past which a kind of foot path conducts to the edge of the bank. The ground is marshy for a considerable space up and down, with a good deal of brushwood scattered about, but part of it had been cutaway from the brow of the precipice, to afford a view of the falls. Turning to the right I followed a narrow path, which skirted the edge of the bank; but stepped slowly and with caution, for I had read alarming accounts of the abundance of rattlesnakes in this quarter. . . . Before reaching the Table Rock, as it is called, at which this path terminates, I stopped behind a few bushes upon a projecting edge, from which I enjoyed a commanding prospect of the wonders before me."

A view of American Falls from Goat Island

Duncan was also curious about one of these features, Table Rock, a sort of shelf that had for years jutted out from the Canadian side of the falls. "During the summer, the American newspapers had announced that the whole of the Table Rock had given way, and been precipitated into the channel of the river; I was therefore eager to ascertain the extent of the mischief. We got over the rail fences of two fields, and passing the distillery to which I have already alluded, reached the edge of the precipice. On looking to the right, I at once remarked the great change which had taken place. From within a few feet of where I stood, the bank which had formerly run forward nearly in a straight line towards the Table Rock, now presented a great concavity. The foot path along which I had formerly walked, and the bushes behind which I had stood, had all disappeared:--the rock upon whose deceitful support they rested, had suddenly given way, from top to bottom, and a mass, as we were informed, about 160 feet in length, and from 30 to 40 in breadth, upon which I had formerly imagined myself in security, now lay shattered into ten thousand fragment sat the bottom of the precipice.... The final disruption of this mass took place about midnight in the month of July or August.... A new path, winding considerably backward from the brow of the cliff, has been cut through the brushwood with which the marsh abounds, and a line of planks conducts the traveler to the Table Rock. The rent extended to within a few yards of this celebrated spot, but no part of it gave way; how long it may be ere it does so, none can say. The top of the Table Rock forms a circular platform of considerable area, on the same level, and in immediate contact, with the western extremity of the British fall. It extends backward for several yards, and I put the point of my shoe into the water, with perfect safety, immediately before it was precipitated from the cliff. In front the rock projects some feet beyond the line of the fall, and of the inferior mass of rocks upon which it is supported; it requires not a little nerve to approach the edge, but the landlord told us that he has seen people sitting with their feet hanging over it, coolly engaged in sketching a view of the falls."

By this time, certain additions had been made to the falls to aid tourists wanting to get from one place to another. However, in a time before safety inspections, these additions were often of questionable stability. Duncan explained, "Leaving the Table Rock we returned by the winding foot path, and a short way below the road from the distillery we reached the ladder, which conducts to the bed of the river. I had imagined that there must be a good deal of danger connected with descending, but on the contrary it is perfectly safe. The top of the ladder is secured between the stumps of two trees, against the side of a deep gash in the rock, and slopes down along the face of the precipice, the lower end resting upon a large accumulation of soil and rock which has formerly fallen from above. There is some difficulty however in getting forward, after having arrived at the foot of the ladder. The path lies to the right along a sloping bank of earth and stones, alternately rising and falling, though ultimately descending as you approach the falls. The footway is so narrow that it admits of no more than one abreast; it is besides wet and slippery throughout, and in many places encumbered with fragments of rock. To look up is frightful; in some places the higher stratum of rock overhangs the rest most threateningly, and the fissures are so numerous, that the whole fabric of the bank seems to be held together by a most precarious cohesion. Your progress is also impeded by the thick rain which is everywhere descending; sometimes filtering through the seams of the rock, sometimes falling in heavy drops from its edge, as from the eaves of a house, and in two or three places spouting upon you in a continued stream. This water proceeds from the marsh above, and by gradually washing out the earth was doubtless the cause of the bank's giving way last summer."

Of course, for most people it was ultimately about the view. In that regard, Duncan wrote, "Various opinions prevail as to the most favourable situation for viewing the falls. Some prefer the road to Chippawa, some the Table Rock, some the rising bank above it, and some the bottom of the precipice. The view from the road to Chippawa is the one which a traveler from Buffalo first obtains; and after the mind has become familiar with the other aspects of the scenery, and can mentally associate what is hid with what is seen, perhaps the circumstance of its having been the first view, may induce him to think it the best. From the Table Rock the spectator has a more complete view of the great fall; commanding at the same time the whole of the furious rapid above, from the first tumultuous roll of the waves, down through its foaming course, till it subsides at the middle of the curve into momentary smoothness, and then dashes below. Here also he has a more appalling impression of the terrors of the scene, for the look from the edge of the rock down into the abyss, is certainly without a parallel. However he is too close upon the great fall, while the one on the American side seems but an episode to the other. From the rising bank above the Table Rock there is perhaps a better grouping of the various features of the landscape; but then you are elevated considerably above the most important objects, a situation which is fatal to powerful impression from objects either of nature or art. At the bottom of the precipice you more adequately appreciate the vastness of the foaming cataracts, their tremendous sound, the terror of the impending precipice, and the boiling of the mighty flood, but to these characteristics your view is confined. The truth is that you must contemplate the scene from every point of view, before you can be acquainted with half its grandeur. Every succeeding look, and every shifting of your position, exhibit something which you did not observe before, and I believe that those who have visited the falls the oftenest, admire and wonder at them the most."

Chapter 5: A Perpetual Creation

"We have not been fortunate in weather, for there cannot be too much, or too warm sunlight for this scene, and the skies have been lowering, with cold, unkind winds. My nerves, too much braced up by such an atmosphere, do not well bear the continual stress of sight and sound. For here there is no escape from the weight of a perpetual creation; all other forms and motions come and go, the tide rises and recedes, the wind, at its mightiest, moves in gales and gusts, but here is really an incessant, an indefatigable motion. Awake or asleep, there is no escape, still this rushing round you and through you. It is in this way I have most felt the grandeur--somewhat eternal, if not infinite. At times a secondary music rises; the cataract seems to seize its own rhythm and sing it over again, so that the ear and soul are roused by a double vibration. This is some effect of the wind, causing echoes to the thundering anthem. It is very sublime, giving the effect of a spiritual repetition through all the spheres." - Sarah Ossoli, June 10, 1843

A circa 1860 picture of a couple with Horseshoe Falls behind them

1841 brought a visit from one of England's most famous author and, at that time, one of England's most famous tourists in America. Charles Dickens toured much of the country, including Niagara Falls, of which he wrote, "Between five and six next morning, we arrived at Buffalo, where we breakfasted; and being too near the Great Falls to wait patiently anywhere else, we set off by the train, the same morning at nine o'clock, to Niagara. It was a miserable day; chilly and raw; a damp mist falling; and the trees in that northern region quite bare and wintry. Whenever the train halted, I listened for the roar and was constantly straining my eyes in the direction where I knew the Falls must be, from seeing the river rolling on towards them; every moment expecting to behold the spray. Within a few minutes of our stopping, not before, I saw two great white clouds rising up slowly and majestically from the depths of the earth. That was all. At length we alighted: and then for the first time, I heard the mighty rush of water, and felt the ground tremble underneath my feet. The bank is very steep, and was slippery with rain, and half melted ice. I hardly know how I got down, but I was soon at the bottom, and climbing, with two English officers who were crossing and had joined me, over some broken rocks, deafened by the noise, half-blinded by the spray, and wet to the skin. We were at the foot of the American Fall. I could see an immense torrent of water tearing headlong down from some great height, but had no idea of shape, or situation, or anything but vague immensity."

Dickens, who was often nothing short of verbose, especially since he was paid by the word, then launched into a monologue akin to a soliloquy detailing the falls' beauty. "When we were seated in the little ferry-boat, and were crossing the swollen river immediately before both cataracts, I began to feel what it was: but I was in a manner stunned, and unable to comprehend the vastness of the scene. It was not until I came on Table Rock, and looked--Great Heaven, on what a fall of bright-green water!--that it came upon me in its full might and majesty. Then, when I felt how near to my Creator I was standing, the first effect, and the enduring one--instant and lasting-- of the tremendous spectacle, was Peace. Peace of Mind: Tranquility: Calm recollections of the Dead: Great Thoughts of Eternal Rest and Happiness: nothing of Gloom or Terror. Niagara was at once stamped upon my heart, an Image of Beauty; to remain there, changeless and indelible, until its pulses cease to beat, forever. Oh, how the strife and trouble of our daily life receded from my view, and lessened in the distance, during the ten memorable days we passed on that Enchanted Ground! What voices spoke from out the thundering water; what faces, faded from the earth, looked out upon me from its gleaming depths; what Heavenly promise glistened in those angels' tears, the drops of many hues, that showered around, and twined themselves about the gorgeous arches which the changing rainbows made! I never stirred in all that time from the Canadian side, whither I had gone at first. I never crossed the river again; for I knew there were people on the other shore, and in such a place it is natural to shun strange company."

Dickens then closed his remarks with what would soon become one of the most oft-quoted descriptions of Niagara Falls. "To wander to and fro all day, and see the cataracts from all points of view; to stand upon the edge of the Great Horse Shoe Fall, marking the hurried water gathering strength as it approached the verge, yet seeming, too, to pause before it shot into the gulf below; to gaze from the river's level up at the torrent as it came streaming down; to climb the neighbouring heights and watch it through the trees, and see the wreathing water in the rapids hurrying onto take its fearful plunge, to linger in the shadow of the solemn rocks three miles below; watching the river as, stirred by no visible cause, it heaved and eddied and awoke the echoes, being troubled yet, far down beneath the surface, by its giant leap; to have Niagara before me, lighted by the sun and by the moon, red in the day's decline, and grey as evening slowly fell upon it; to look upon it every day, and wake up in the night and hear its ceaseless voice: this was enough. I think in every quiet season now, still do those waters roll and leap, and roar and tumble, all day long; still are the rainbows spanning them, a hundred feet below. Still, when the sun is on them, do they shine and glow like molten gold. Still, when the day is gloomy, do they fall like snow, or seem to crumble away like the front of a great chalk cliff, or roll adown the rock like dense white smoke. But always does the mighty stream appear to die as it comes down, and always from its unfathomable grave arises that tremendous ghost of spray and mist which is never laid: which has haunted this place with the same dread solemnity since Darkness brooded on the deep, and that first flood before the Deluge--Light--came rushing on Creation at the word of God."

When former President John Quincy Adams visited the falls two years later, he said in a speech before those present with him at the falls that day, "You have what no other nation on earth has.

At your very door there is a mighty cataract--one of the most wonderful works of God. I have passed through the seventh and nearly half of the eighth decade of life, and yet, until a few days ago, I had known of the cataract only by name and the common fame of the historian. But now I have seen it! Yes, I have seen it in all its sublimity and glory--and I have never witnessed a scene its equal. I experience the same feeling in your presence as when I saw it--there is left in my mind a deep impression which will last with my life--a feeling overpowering, and which takes away the power of speech by its grandeur and sublimity, contrasted with the eddying river above, the rippling current below, and the rainbow, a pledge of God to mankind that the destruction from the waters shall not again visit the earth. I say, altogether it takes away language as well as thought: and in this enraptured condition one is almost capable of prophesying --standing as it were in a trance, unable to speak.... I have been at Lundy's Lane and at Chippewa.... I have seen no memento of that political era between these two countries--divided by that natural phenomenon between the two, as if heaven had considered it too much for one. There I have been received as a friend with friendly greeting, and I ejaculate a prayer to God, that this state of temper may be perpetual, and that the land of war and of garments rolled in blood may never again be exhibited."

A few years later, in 1848, the unusually cold winter caused the falls to freeze over entirely, slowing the waters that normally poured over them to a mere trickle. Downstream, factories that were dependent on the power of the swift waters passing through their waterwheels were forced to shut down until the mighty falls thawed out. When that happened again in 1911, *The Buffalo Express* would report, "The Falls of Niagara can be compared to nothing but a mere mill dam this morning. In the memory of the oldest inhabitants, never was there so little water running over Niagara's awful precipice, as at this moment! Hundreds of people are now witnessing that which never has, and probably never may again be witnessed on the Niagara River. Last night at 11 o'clock the factories fed from the waters of this majestic river were in full operation, and at 12 o'clock the water was shut off, the wheels suddenly ceased their revolutions, and everything was hushed into silence."

By the 1840s, the area around the falls had become well settled, and people who lived in the area began to demand a way of moving back and forth across the water. In 1846, both the state of New York and the Government of Upper Canada approved the formation of two bridge companies, the Niagara Falls Suspension Bridge Company of Canada and the International Bridge Company of New York, and these two companies together would build and operate a bridge.

In 1847, the companies commissioned engineer Charles Ellet, Jr., who had gained fame through the construction of the world's first cable suspension bridge across the Schuylkill River in Pennsylvania, to build a suspension bridge across the river. One man wrote, "The Suspension Bridge at Niagara Falls is a most sublime work of art - it is impossible to give a clear idea of the grandeur of the work. Imagine a bridge 800 feet in length hung in the air, at the height of 230 feet, over a vast body of water rushing through a narrow gorge at the rate of thirty miles an hour. To a spectator below it looks like a strip of paper suspended by a cobweb. When the wind is strong, the frail gossamer-looking structures ways to and fro as if ready to start from its fastenings, and it shakes from extremity to centre at the firm tread of a pedestrian. But there is no danger -- men pass over it with perfect safety while the head of the timid looker-on swims with apprehension."

Ellet

The bridge companies soon realized that the area needed to be served by a railway, and that a new bridge to carry the railway across the river was necessary. In 1853, the companies approved a design by the famous architect John Augustus Roebling for a bridge to accommodate the Grand Trunk Railway to connect Canada and the United States. This bridge was completed in 1855.

By this time, the Niagara Falls Hydraulic Power and Mining Company had built a number of canals designed to redirect the water in the falls in order to drive the motors of nearby factories. According to a pamphlet published in 1854, "The canal commences at a point on the Niagara

River about half a mile above the rapids, and is to be carried to a point about one fourth of a mile below the Falls, where it will terminate in a basin, from which the waters may be discharged at pleasure over the perpendicular bank before mentioned. Its entire length will not exceed three fourths of a mile. It is to be seventy feet in width by ten feet in depth, and it is estimated that it will maintain a running stream equal in quantity to 2436 cubic feet per second. ... The "anchor ice," which in winter chokes the race so as to impede the machinery for weeks, can never form in the proposed canal ; and the perpetual moisture caused by the falling spray, so destructive to wooden work and otherwise fruitful of trouble and loss to manufacturers, will also cease to be a source of annoyance."

The years following the Civil War saw the New York Central railroad complete its first line to the falls, bringing with it yet another bridge, but more importantly, Niagara Falls began to generate electricity. In 1881, a man named Jacob Schoellkopf built the first of several hydroelectric generating stations at the falls, and the energy came from the water that constantly fell more than 80 feet into the devices set to harvest its power. A few years later, one author observed, "It is well known among leading manufacturers in the United States that the water-power heretofore available is steadily diminishing as the country becomes more thickly settled. At many places in the Eastern States it has become necessary to supplement the water-power with steam in order to be able to run machinery during the entire twenty-four hours, thereby greatly increasing the cost of production. Most of the water-power in use in various sections of the country has been produced by the construction, at great cost, of dams for the storage of water during the dry season. These devices have at times proved inadequate to supply the water required for manufacturing purposes, and at other times, when freshets prevailed, the dams have given way, depriving the manufacturing establishments of power, and inflicting great damage upon the adjacent country. ... At Niagara Nature has built an imperishable dam from the solid rock, which she maintains without cost to man, so that the manufacturer who avails himself of its power is relieved, from the beginning, of all anxiety about his dams ever giving way and causing death and destruction of property. He is also assured that his mills can never stand idle for lack of water, because, instead of being dependent upon some slender and fickle stream, he draws his copious supply from the mammoth reservoirs which constitute the Great Chain of Lakes. There will, therefore, be nothing to interrupt the steady flow of the manufacturer's yearly production at the minimum of cost."

The next major improvement to Niagara Falls' generating capacity came in 1895 when Westinghouse Electric completed the Adams Power Plant Transformer House. The following year, several 19th century moguls, including the Vanderbilt's and the Astor's, teamed up to build a series of tunnels that would direct the water to giant turbines capable of generating up to 100,000 horsepower.

With that infrastructure in place, the main concern was how to use the vast power being generated. *Scientific American* observed in 1899, "In the few years that have intervened since the water was first turned into the wheel-pit of the Niagara Falls Power Plant, a large number of entirely new industries have sprung up around, or within easy touch of, the station ; while establishments that were already existing have become extensive users of the power. That the tendency is for the industries to gravitate to the power rather than the power to be transmitted to the industries is shown by the fact that out of a total of 35,000 horse power delivered from the station, over three-fourths are consumed in its vicinity, as against less than one-fourth that is transmitted to a distance — the principal long distance transmission being that of 8,000 horse power to Buffalo, for the use of the Cataract Power and Conduit Company. Although the natural trend of events, controlled by well understood economic laws, has brought about a centralization of industries at the falls, it is not to be inferred that long distance transmission will not enter largely into the ultimate utilization of the energy of Niagara. In the few years since construction was first started a great stride has been made in art of generating and manipulating electrical currents for transmission, and the remarkable installation recently opened in Southern California, here a transmission of 83 miles has been successfully accomplished, suggests that a large part of the 74 millions of hydraulic horse power available at the falls may yet be transformed and transmitted to the large cities of the East. The present indications are, however, that for some time to come transmissions are not likely to be attempted for distances of over 100 miles. The difficulties are not now so much of a physical nature (thanks to the alternating current of high potential), but are largely economical—the great cost of the line rapidly offsetting the cheap cost of production at the power station."

Soon, the Canadian government joined the power generating business, completing a number of power generating stations on its side of the falls during the early 1900s.

Chapter 6: The Whirlwind of Spray

"We paused almost in front of a branch of the Fall and tried to look up; but so blinding was the whirlwind of spray that we could hardly see. The cavern was washed out by the wash of ages. A huge sheet of water, a stupendous curtain of force, so thick that its transparent drops were massed into a translucent wall, fell beside us. It was so thick, so dense, so immense that we could barely see the beams of light through that massive veil of water. The spray filled our eyes, hung upon our lashes, ran down our noses until we tried to gasp out that we had seen enough; and gladly turned away. The sound was deafening; we could not hear one another speak. The spray was too great to allow us to see anything, and yet this was only a small branch of the Falls themselves. It gave a wonderful idea of what the hourly, weekly, monthly, yearly overflow of those Falls, which Goat Island divides, must be. 'Please walk this way,' said our guide, and into a long, dark passage, with a tiny gleam of light at the end, we went." - Mrs. Alec Tweedie, author of *America As I Saw It* (1913)

As a result, Niagara Falls was serving two major purposes by the end of the 19th century. In addition to generating vast amounts of electrical power, Niagara Falls was being promoted regularly as the perfect spot for vacationers or honeymooners to visit. A brochure published in

1890 told readers, "Thanks to the energies of Lord Dufferin, then Governor- General of Canada, and Governor Robinson of New York, parks on either side have been opened up free to the public. The Suspension Bridge which is crossed by the Southern (Great Western) Division of the Grand Trunk is one of the engineering triumphs of the age. It has a span of 1,230 feet from tower to tower, and the floor is 256 feet above the water level. This bridge was opened January 1, 1869; it is a two-storied structure, the upper story being used for the purposes of the Grand Trunk Railway, and the bottom story for foot and passenger traffic."

In 1897, the Whirlpool Rapids Bridge, made entirely of steel, was completed closer to the falls, allowing tourists to pass across it between Canada and the United States.

A picture of the Upper Steel Arch Bridge

An early 20th century picture of the falls

Following the end of World War One, people grew more concerned about protecting Niagara Falls for its natural beauty. One writer reported, "In the past quarter of a century, great strides have been made in geological science, notwithstanding which, the goal of certain knowledge about the age of Niagara has not yet been reached. Very naturally, geological knowledge concerning Niagara has not developed in geological order. Recent and more obvious evidence has attracted first attention, while the remote and fundamental problems have received later consideration. Inquiries proceeding from effect to cause have led backward to antecedents and formative events, with the result that while many correct observations and valuable discoveries of existing facts have been made from time to time,--as, for instance, the drift-filled channel of St. David's or the submerged valleys of Lake Ontario--the original theories of the causes of these conditions have been upset by the later discoveries of other investigators. Thus it has been that pioneers who have been correct in their observations have been incorrect in their theories, and followers who possibly have had correct theories have benefited by the observations of their predecessors. Many of the early observers of the physical phenomena of Niagara gave much attention to the formation of mists, rainbows, sound, the color of the water, the upward jets beneath the Falls, etc. Triangulation and surveys of the crest have proceeded with increasing accuracy since about 1838. The height of the Falls, stated by Father Hennepin in his amazement to be 600 feet, was ascertained with approximate accuracy as early as 1805 to be 158 feet, and in recent years has been fixed by the United States Geological Survey at 160 feet for the Horseshoe Fall. The volume of the river was a subject of speculation in 1805, when it was estimated at 3,000,000 tons. Another estimate at the same period was 400,000 tons as the weight of the mass between the crest and bottom of the Falls. In 1882, it was estimated that from 85,000,000 to

102,000,000 tons of water passed in an hour. But this branch of the subject merges into the hydraulic and industrial use of the Falls, which is discussed elsewhere in this work."

In 1941, as World War II in Europe drew America and Canada closer together, the Niagara Falls Bridge Commission completed the Rainbow Bridge, which allowed people on foot and cars to easily cross between the two countries. In addition to that, changes were made to the way in which the water flows to the falls; in 1955, some of the area between Goat Island and the edge of the bank of the river was filled in to create Terrapin Point.

In 1956, Niagara Falls experienced one of its most traumatic setbacks when a rock slide severely damaged its largest hydropower station. This tragedy, and the jobs lost as factories stood silent, led Congress to pass the Niagara Redevelopment Act, which "directs and authorizes the Commission to issue a license to the Power Authority for a project with the capacity to use all of the United States' share of Niagara River water available for power generation. The Niagara Redevelopment Act provides that the license is to include specific conditions pertaining to distribution of project power, rates, transmission, and other matters. These specified conditions are "in addition to those deemed necessary and required under the terms of the [FPA]. ... [and] establishes certain requirements with respect to any license issued by the Commission to the Power Authority for the Niagara Project. With regard to allocation of project power, Niagara Redevelopment Act section 836 provides: (1) that the license shall require the Power Authority to make at least 50 percent of the project power available to public bodies and 33 Reservoir State Park, Niagara Gorge, and ArtPark. ... non-profit cooperatives for the purpose of ensuring that the power is sold to consumers at the lowest rates reasonably possible (referred to as "preference power"); and (2) that a reasonable portion (up to 20 percent) of the power that could be allocated as preference power is to be made available for use within neighboring states."

In 1958, construction began on the largest power plant to date to be driven by the Niagara Falls. Though it took five years to complete, it was able to begin generating power by 1961. Lou Paonessa, once the community affairs director for the New York Power Authority, said of the men who built it, "They're like a brotherhood. They accomplished something that could never be done today. They built the power plant in three years, from first dig to first power." Charles Cowart, one of the laborers, added, "This venture will live on forever."

In 1969, the United States Army Corps of Engineers had to dam up the falls so it could clear out some rock from the base. For some time, the area around the falls had been plagued by rock slides, and the engineers also used that time to make some much needed repairs to the American side of the falls. After four years of being diverted to the Canadian side of the falls, normal flows were restored in November 1969.

A picture of the American Falls dammed in 1969

Chapter 7: Stunts

A scene depicting Harry Houdini swimming near Niagara Falls in *The Man from Beyond* (1922)

While most people come to Niagara Falls to see nature in action, others have viewed it as a challenge. In fact, for hundreds of years, people have seen the falls as a place for daredevil adventures.

One of the first men to publicly try to go over the falls was Sam Patch, who survived a jump from a tower to the gorge below in 1829.

On October 24, 1901, Annie Edson Taylor, then 63, began the tradition of going over Niagara Falls in a barrel, even though she admitted after her adventure, "No one ought ever do that again." The next day the *New York Times* reported, "A widowed woman, Mrs. Anna Edson Taylor, safely passed over Niagara Falls in a barrel this afternoon. The trip from end to end was witnessed by several thousand people. ...It was beyond any conception but her own that she would live to tell the story. But she is alive to-night, and the doctors say as soon as she gets over the shock she will be all right. This initial voyage over Niagara's cataract began at Port Day, nearly a mile from the brink of the Falls. From Port Day Mrs. Taylor and her barrel were taken out to Grass Island, where she entered the barrel, and at 3:50 she was in tow of a boat speeding well out into the Canadian current. At 4:05 the barrel was set adrift, and Mrs. Taylor was at the mercy of currents in waters that never before have been known to spare a human life once in its grasp. From the spot where the rowboat left the barrel the current runs frightfully swift and soon breaks over the reefs that cause the water to toss in fury. The barrel was weighted with 200-pound anvil, and it floated nicely in the water, Mrs. Taylor apparently retaining an upright position for the greater part of the trip down the river and through the rapids. ... It dropped over the fall at 4:23 o'clock, the bottom well down. In less than a minute it appeared at the base of the fall, and was swept down stream. The current cast it aside in an eddy, and, floating back up stream, it was held between two eddies until captured at 4:40 o'clock. As it was landed on a rock out in the river it was difficult to handle, but several men soon had the hatch off. Mrs. Taylor was alive and conscious, but before she could be taken out of the barrel it was necessary to saw a portion of the top away. Her condition was a surprise to all. She walked along the shore to a boat, and was taken down the river to the Maid of the Mist Dock, where she entered a carriage and was brought to this city."

Taylor and her barrel

While she survived, Taylor did not get away unscathed. The article continued, "She is suffering greatly from the shock. She has a three-inch cut in her scalp back of the right ear, but how or when she got it she does not know. She complains of pain between the shoulders, but this is thought to be from the fact that her shoulders were thrown back during the plunge, as she had her arms in straps, and these undoubtedly save her nick from breaking. In passing over the falls she admits having lost consciousness. While thanking God for sparing her life, she warns everybody against trying to make the trip. So severe was the shock that she wanders in her talk, but there is little doubt but that she will be in good condition within a day or two. … The barrel in which Mrs. Taylor made the journey is 4 1/2 feet high and about 3 feet in diameter. A leather harness and cushions inside protected her body. Air was secured through a rubber tube connected with a small opening near the top of the barrel."

Since Taylor's trip, 14 others people have deliberately gone over the falls inside various containers, but not all of them have survived. Some have even made the leap with nothing more than a life preserver to protect them. Dozens of people are killed going over Niagara Falls each year, but most of them are suicides.

Bobby Leach and his steel barrel in 1911

Other daredevils preferred to make names for themselves without getting wet. During the latter half of the 19th century, a number of tightrope walkers made successful trips across various areas around the falls, though never over the actual Falls themselves. Among these high wire artists was Maria Spelterini who, at the age of 23 in 1876, became the only woman to successfully cross the falls on a tightrope. Two decades later, in 1896, such escapades were outlawed, but the famous daredevil Nik Wallenda did the stunt in 2012 after receiving special permission from both the American and Canadian governments to do so.

A picture of Maria Spelterini doing the stunt in 1876

Chapter 8: Recent History

Ujjwal Kumar's picture of American and Bridal Veil Falls

Ujjwal Kumar's picture of Horseshoe Falls

Niagara Falls is one of America's most iconic natural wonders, and it has drawn millions of people over the centuries, but the aspects of it that inspire so much awe also make conservation more difficult. In 2014, the Niagara Escarpment Legacy Project described the falls and their surroundings: "The Niagara Escarpment, as it transects Niagara County along an east to west path on a narrow strip of dramatic, 150-foot-high rock outcroppings, is known worldwide as a geological marvel. But there is so much more to it than geology. In this report you will learn that the Niagara Escarpment is also a treasure trove of ecological diversity, a scenic wonder, and a living history exhibit — a jewel in our midst. The escarpment holds flora, fauna, fossils, soils, waterways, and wetlands in an astonishing variety for so small an area of land, existing in a host of ecological communities, some especially noteworthy such as the potential for oak openings, alvar shrubland, and alvar woodland communities. You will also find species that have been recognized by New York State and by scientists as threatened and of special concern."

The authors of the project went on to add, "Our Project will explain how, over the centuries, the Niagara Escarpment has played host to human activities from groups as varied as Native Americans, European settlers, armies, escaping African- American slaves, farmers, manufacturers, entrepreneurs, miners, and commercial shippers. Despite the constant and sometimes destructive activity of its human inhabitants and visitors, the escarpment has shown itself to be forgiving, resilient, and constantly awe-inspiring. However, this report will explain that the escarpment needs careful stewardship if it is to remain such a valuable and timeless resource."

In explaining what they were studying, the team wrote, "The Niagara Escarpment in Niagara County is part of an international escarpment that stretches 750 miles from central New York, west across the Niagara River and Niagara Falls, northwest through Ontario, up the Bruce Peninsula and onto Manitoulin Island, into Michigan's Upper Peninsula, leveling out eventually in Wisconsin. The escarpment is the steep north face of a bedrock ridge whose sedimentary rock layers were formed from sediments deposited more than 400 million years ago when North American was closer to the equator and the escarpment region was covered by a shallow sea. The ridge we see today is the result of tectonic uplift, multiple glaciations, and millions of years of erosion. The climatic and geological features that define the ecology, history, and economy of this region, including the formation of the Niagara Gorge and Niagara Falls, have been influenced by the escarpment. The escarpment traps warmer air along the southern shore of Lake Ontario, creating unique microclimates that are ideal for fruit tree farms and vineyards, and the steep terrain, rock-strewn slopes, and deeply incised creek valleys of the escarpment itself create habitat types and plant and animal communities that include mature forests, savannahs, grassland habitats, vernal pools, talus caves, cool, moist glades, and transitional shrub habitats. The geology, fossil diversity, and ecology of the Niagara Escarpment have drawn the attention of the United Nations, which recognized the Canadian portion as a Biosphere Reserve in 1990."

In the end, the project concluded, "Conservation, preservation, restoration — three words that have appeared often in the preceding pages — define the most important word in this report's title: "Legacy." Tucked into the lengthy pages of scientific field survey results, social history, strategies, and goals is an underlying message: the Niagara Escarpment deserves to be the legacy that we leave to future generations. Formed from bedrock eons ago, and now the sturdy host to richly populated ecological communities of a broad biodiversity, this geologic marvel is still susceptible to irreversible damage by unfettered development, poorly considered land use, and an invasion of unwanted species. If this study has been successful, it will have shown all the stakeholders — from individuals who simply enjoy the peace of a public park to landowners, governments, not-for-profit organizations, tourists, citizens of residential areas, history buffs. Native Americans, farmers, leaders of commerce and industry — that protection of the escarpment is in everyone's common interest."

Behind Horseshoe Falls

Online Resources

Other titles about Niagara Falls

The Grand Canyon: The History of the America's Most Famous Natural Wonder by Charles River Editors

Yosemite National Park: The History of California's Most Famous Park by Charles River Editors

Yellowstone National Park: The History of America's Most Famous Park by Charles River

Editors

Bibliography

Berton, Pierre (2009). *Niagara: A History of the Falls*. State University of New York Press.

Grant, Grant; Ray Jones (2006). *Niagara Falls : an intimate portrait*. Insiders/Globe Pequot.

McGreevy, Patrick (2009). *Imagining Niagara: The Meaning and Making of Niagara Falls*. Univ of Massachusetts.

Made in the USA
San Bernardino, CA
09 August 2017